HOUSES

POEMS BY NIKKI

WALLSCHLAEGER

Houses

HORSE LESS PRESS

PUBLISHED BY HORSE LESS PRESS IN GRAND RAPIDS, MI / HORSELESSPRESS. ORG / COPYRIGHT © 2015 NIKKI WALLSCHLAEGER / ALL RIGHTS RESERVED / ISBN 978-0-9908139-3-4 / COVER PHOTO BY BRIAN WALLSCHLAEGER / BACK COVER PHOTO BY NIKKI WALLSCHLAEGER / LAYOUT AND DESIGN OF COVERS BY BRIAN WALLSCHLAGER / DESIGN CONCEPT FOR PHOTOS BY NIKKI WALLSCHLAEGER / INTERIOR DESIGN AND COMPOSITION BY ALBAN FISCHER / SET IN BERTHOLD AKZIDENZ GROTESK, FILOSOFIA, AND HEROE / PRINTED IN THE UNITED STATES OF AMERICA / FIRST EDITION

FOR MILES, BRIAN, & SAGE

"Perhaps home is not a place but simply an irrevocable condition."

—JAMES BALDWIN

"The art of feeling at home with the most uncanny of all guests."

—TIQQUN

HOUSES

Pink House

Pink houses are nice. A nice house. A red worm shitting berries. A baby magnolia tree. A homing marrow. An arduous alley twirl. New pink hightops, we have a new neighbor. A colony of mottled ants. A busty shoelace. A bus is breaking a beep. A comb of car plumes, with or without highstepper. He said if I was 30 years younger he would be sayin hello. Pink leather seat on a motorcycle. An underwire bra I'm going to repair so I shove you on top or bottom drawer.

A nice yard with a firepit. A baked chicken. An old whiskey barrel grunting. Pink little farms teased up and down your arms. Sailboats, of course. We dream about sailboats. And tugboats as red as knees, chameleon lay. He says I basilisk in the sun, blackish tongue w/ a pink lady apple, walking to the bus stop. Chalked croup hearts on the boarded up pink house. A possible home. A cat with a kitten whine. Dandelion greens for supper. Creeping charlie curving around my ankles, a purple canella teat,

Certainly a homebody. Certainly an estranged somebody, tearing pink in the spring. I cannot post how flowers yell, but how was my baby's day at school? Brown /pink cheeks of children weather. A crisis messed mother, but moving right along. Vote tropes of the same old hopes. Girls blogging a picture of a displaced koala. Seagull salon overheard. And a nice house for you, a pink house, two family house, nice yard, a chokecherry tree in back for the kids to climb.

Red House

Not a schoolhouse for quaint-ification purposes, commemoration toward stationery seal. Not a genius either, a manhandling splice. La Cucaracha is a family friendly horn call and the owner of the car is pleased. I am pleased that he is pleased. That's the point. Not a dye of fish patty per each Orwellian.

Not a daughters of the revolution firetruck with a stuffed dalmatian knight rider, so the traffic of peeps past my house talk & sing. It's an urgent delivery past the concept of property lineage. Not the town and country quirky set spanking missionary style soufflés. Not the gaff bell that frolics with the constitution.

Not a focal point in the age of crust. An old madhouse is my self-esteem because the disinheritance is my inheritance. Not an Edith Wharton bookmark arranged in Trafalgar square for impulse fallout of a movement slogan. Not the Mason-Dixon trunk show for Clydesdale gallery night. Gallery as gallows.

Not the patent leather seagull for a breast gene. The old boys love a girl for the old monopoly skin graft. My birth certificate proves that I can be taxed for buying labor supplies. Not my mother's indignation either, an online junk store. The point is presidents age by exchanging juried price tags. They like to win.

Yellow House

As a westerner, I will only paint thinking about Matisse. As a westerner, your poverty is romantic. As a westerner, overpopulation is the cause and not the effect. As a westerner, legwork is a numb strut.

As a westerner, I will want to leave my country. As a westerner, my mother will make an American out of me. As a westerner, fair trade coffee is always epic. As a westerner, the wars are guaranteed.

As a westerner, I will cook popcorn sentimentality in the microwave. As a westerner, I will throw popcorn to the pigeons at a central park. As a westerner, I am efficient in global news inflections.

As a westerner, I will sneer at your first world problems. As a westerner, I will use the best bridesmaid agency in town. As a westerner, I will pretend to have an accent. As a westerner, I will be bawse.

As a westerner, I will desire open—air markets. As a westerner, happy hours are pub crawls. As a westerner, condoms and education will solve everything. As a westerner, I was raised Catholic.

As a westerner, I will love all peoples. As a westerner, I will flirt with eating disorders. As a westerner I will vote for a Democratic president. As a westerner, I will wear limited edition sarcoline pumps.

As a westerner, I will study international relations. As a westerner, I will teach displaced families how to make s'mores. As a westerner, I will be proud of the family crest. As a westerner, I take back the night.

As a westerner, I will approve of celebrity activists. As a westerner, I preordered for Gatsby. As a westerner, I will have astigmatism from combat insignia. As a westerner, I 'm not looking at you

Orange House

A long world on a long street on a long boulevard covered with oranges, & I know they can't grow here, oranges, but here is an orange blossom in the middle of my skirt & what I thought was jasmine is a wish less desperate, a tiger lily sticking out hir tongue in the heat , learning how to write a protest novel.

A long poster hanging in the long kitchen of my cervix, the one I painted hanging on an old wall, indwelling with star breath not automata, his head resting on my waist afterwards. We both hear it. Someone, a long way off. He's waiting quietly, a hooded oculist, in a pup tent on the national lawn.

A long dress before a wedding on the long night before, walking barefoot in the French quarter with a priestess and a band of slim men w/ beards drumming, one year before houses, young & old, went missing or left for Texas. He was such a rotten president, a dark of overconfidence, pizza vomit.

A long faced man, he is a woodworker who keeps his own long hours, in another plashy city but this one free of cars & gamely plastered with sexy drawers as we look for lunch. I am a gondolier from a family of gondoliers, he said, it's a tradition, a creative tradition, for us to navigate what you take for granted.

Green House

Steam house. Spring before grass cutters, the best time. Thick before drought and angry man management, he must gut the grass on the weekends, imagine the scandal if not. What will the neighbors think, I think nothing. Don't bother. Don't bother the sod, push mower. Go green with upcycled link purses, I am that auctioneer w/ other epidurals made possible to me in part by gas.

So he gets out his lawn mower anyway, paints his house in acceptable olive, not green, green like new grass, that would be too confrontational, too many risks of dandelion patty cake. City citation says no food gardens allowed on front lawns, city citation says I can't puff naked across my lawn. What will the neighbors think about my hairs. Maybe you shouldn't be bothered by looking.

Nonsense, says man in powdered bone who believes in modified tomatoes, but green tomatoes are good. Without his placards. Behind the scenes people make recipes out of green things, make livings out of weeds wild and cultivated just so, hidden somewhere. No dogs allowed in the secret counties, you have to know someone. Would angry man tell on the guerillas of green feet? Maybe so, maybe not

Maybe he tried it in college and now offhandedly works networking parties playing I don't know what a bong is. We laugh. Oh, how we laugh and the quotas brighten, the death rows roll and the afternoon tea swells. Someone is getting arrested and grocery stores flash with broccoli. She is wearing a green house scarf as an American doing the foreign thing in an African country she was briefed on during the flight.

Black House

Invisible house. Flowers up in front, children sittin on the porch, he gets picked up every day to go to therapy, he has to get the other leg cut off now. What they call it? When you can still feel what isn't supposed to be there? My legs have been botherin me in the dampness, and he always thought I was a little funny because I moved in with a white man and obviously wasn't from here.

I sits at my invisible house. My grandma also talks that way, somewhat, she was from the country some ways back but she raised me and when we went to value village, she was practically the only white lady in there. She polka glowed when she told the checkout lady I was her granddaughter. the lady smiled like she was amused, but gently kindly. She likes to hold my hand when we cross the street

so people wondered. They stare at us from their monster salvaged pin-up trucks with collectible plate gullets. Sedans, too, painted safe parking lot colors so you could get lost w/a cart full of groceries, little fobs of baby food that spliff in the tin of your gland. Night camping at noon. What they call it? That place the other poet talked about, fog or no headlights, room temperature, a low-grade fever from bologna,

it's possible if my elite panic was framed in blacklight they would be coerced into box office seating . I should take a picture before the cattle adrenals finally revoke the lacing of my lavender, and I think his small town bobby socks are the new security code to get into the vomitorium. Also fake military service records. Cops get to go on special paid leave when they murder here. You gotta be careful nowadays.

Grey House

Cartoon house. Animated house. By the creators of, mapped to you by. Sponsored by something and chump, houses by the pound. Soldiers coming home from the big wars to reservation and ghetto. Grey duplex and desert roses secretly revived with grandmother names. Labored breathing. Blues chants.

Holes in the ground. Prairie dogs in earthen tunnels safe from the sun. Old weather wet teddy bears tied to the lampposts, color all gone, rain ran away with the shovel to unbury the living stuck. Detroit City stuffing. HUD houses leaking with tunnel-grey wind, slate sidewalks engraved w/little hand casings.

Animated jail cell house. Notice how the bars are usually wide enough to sneak prisoners through. Entertainment is cheap for men returning home. Sit on the couch. Cold steel bootstraps to slip through past sleeping toons. Men in uniform refuse service to other men in uniform. Spittle on the screen.

Commodity lawns we pass on the highway. Cinereal ash from old volcanoes & people upheaval, now marked in white cross tatter, or limy platinum. Burial is expensive. She needs to save in her old age because the check don't stretch that way, into national plumbing, a likely cause of elderberry death.

White House

This is the place. High magic, she said. That's what they're doin, & it's not the good kind, either. Old plantation times movin over my wrist, the shadow of this famous fence. How would it feel if the clouds were owned, if they finally figured out how to escape the weather? Somewhere, I think in Mississippi, are the boarded up bones of my women kin, but I believe all of their spirits are really being held hostage in the secret tombs of our nation's capital, concentrated into the first lady's gems with other folks, too.

Everything that has ever happened to our people on this continent has been recorded. When I say recorded, I don't necessarily mean with ledgers & fountain pens & scriptures & all of that pearly shit, although some of it is, except most folks don't really understand what these stories are trying to say because they are categorized as "art" or "literature" or "gospel" which is part of the deflection process, the process of peeling people apart from themselves. There's always a big knife in the kitchen.

Our people sure have strong arms, she said. Those Ionic columns forced to hold up that cotton pickin house. That's why the white house gets repainted every year, they're afraid the cracks will show. Black cracks. Where the skid plate is getting desperate. Before most of us could learn their chicken scratch we left other things

Blue
House

A blue house where water is responsible for all of our thinkings. In the desert water is choosy, in the oases the palms are large and loud, chatter, piss, food. Clatter, room, lick. Sit on the toilet and read to me while I'm in the tub.

I sit and rub the cat who licks from the faucet, she prefers water to be running into her, not placid meniscus like a dog pillow by the fireplace. He sleeps without frills, in the water bubble, but plenty of cat paws cat heads we ask politely to leave the room

afterwards we read the diaper papers of our times. Warm feather water eased by pain and window of fogged glass blocks, you can hear the mens walking by. Once in a while we will hear someone say I saw something it's a bathroom

it's a bathroom window, a naked woman hope, being all hawt, hair pinned up. An agreeable romance cutting through the yard but no, it's usually you or me or the young un playing with blue dinghys and splashing bumble trucks I say did you wash your

body properly with the washrag I gave you. Here are your pajamas it's time to go to bed now that you are damp from your bath maybe you'll dream about tadpoles.

Violet House

When you start moving your mouth like a baby's again, it's time to go into the house and find the blueberries I left in the icebox. So he made a map of her country. In pen, I saw the truth of its neglect and the truth of her exhaustion. She hesitated before I wrote the word, "truth."So there's a window, & it's a typical window. It's got rain smeared across it, which is also typical, or maybe snow, depending on the time of year. There's an older lady walking around, and he makes these certain noises I could conjure in the deepest of sleep, especially when I gets up from his chair

by the window. She rocks in this chair. I rocks me. He often watches her rocking, and I know on some level she is drawing power. The phone is next to him in case it rings because I knows when it will ring. The chair changes colors & patterns so she doesn't fade into the fabric. So this one night the older lady is in his chair, sitting in the room with her daughter who is in a chair that tilts back into the brown paneled wall. This chair remains, through the years, the same shade of country rose, although a white crocheted throw appears on the scene one year after the daughter rests on the back of my neck.

It is rare that the daughter is in for the night- no work, no dates. He's reading yesterday's newspapers so I must be playing catch up. She wants to know what I thinks he missed. So there's this room connected to the room where they are all doing evening things. It is dark & shadowy in this room, everyone calls it the dining room even though they rarely eat around the oak table covered with tambourines. In order to get to the bathroom I plays a game.

She pretends it's a rare bird of lava, a burning cow, the square marked go
starts by her mother's chair. If he falls in, she will forget me. I won't angle
his car in the driveway anymore after her shift at the tavern downtown &
It's like when my grandmother gets out the ice tool and breaks up the ice.
It melts in the gutter and becomes a run for ants. So he made a map of
her family. In pen, she saw the truth of their neglect and the truth of her
exhaustion. He hesitated even longer before she wrote the word, "truth."

Gold House

There are lions and the shoppers are looking for them because we live in a mall, following the groupon panic of our neighbors.

There is no small talk anymore. There's still warmth, but in a distracted silly-string sort of skeeball way. That's to be expected.

We're figuring out how we got here in the first place. A song from an '80s supergroup says the same damn thing. It's a real pleasure to meet you.

I recently figured out how I can tell when someone is trying to pull rank. They either shorten your name or pretend you don't have one.

Brown House

A single brown curtain that separated his room from the rest of the house. He was not a man behind the unwashed curtain type.

I don't know who gave him that curtain but I'm guessing it was grandma. She probably made it herself while watching 60 minutes. I sat nearby, reading a Babysitter's Club book. Claudia Kishi was my favorite

since she wore the coolest clothes. Deliriously printed leggings and palm tree-t shirts. She also hid junk food in her room and painted celebratory still-lives of them whenever her parents weren't looking.

Like me, she was also terrible at math and needed a tutor. I remember my mother getting frustrated when she tried to help me, but he was content to watch Bonanza in the late afternoon.

He liked to drink Pepsi and for Christmas, my aunt and uncle would wrap up a 12-pack of Pepsi for him to open because everyone assumed he had given up on everything else. It was a cruel inside joke.

Mint Green House

This is where my great grandma lived. We're both wearing minkettes for the family funny farm portrait. Say cheese America! We're eating watermelons.

Denied entry into the building where everyone gets in through the back door. A shelter built for the park. There's a desk. He's eating Judge's famous potato salad.

Whoever organized this reunion is relying on our compliance to play dumb. So we organize a game of ironic field hockey. If someone wanted to kill us it would be so easy.

I don't feel safe but I work in a federal building. After all is said and done, isn't gangsta rap just the shadow of the shadow? Me and my NWA t-shirt, far left.

Silver House

Tressed & mussed by the stars that sing about stars. My motown vacation bats me around while the moon watched the city die.

When the city dies, the garden erupts. The avenues are not crowded, so we watch each other before s/he fills herself with old light, which is not nostalgia. We're using the past instead of letting it use us.

When the past uses us, it means we need to go to sleep for awhile. That is not always good. We must sleep in shifts so we each have a turn to rest for the next moon beat,

when the next moon comes we better watch for cops. I will cover myself w/ a blanket in the meantime, tending to others. Our night sweats bring active listening to the community

the community who sleeps so the city becomes what we don't recollect so we call it death. This is poor dream autophony when everything is about rent

death is not everything. It's not the moon. That's the past, being user friendly bringing the blankets made for safe sleeping. The people sleeping in shifts inspect for smallpox

smallpox not what we dream but they are good knitters. Gets in the way of deciding how to crash, like all billowing metaphors, trinkets, beams, ideas about light, snow all the flings we remember in a crowded ballroom on an avenue twisted w/ cops. It was a cold dream night for July so I am going to kiss my friends good fight

while the next moon comes, the old fixed light crowding out, the city rot lying, dressed & fussed by the death gardens we sleep, dreaming of non-continuity

Bronze
House

Statues in the concession gardens until the beachmaster hippo signaled
it was time to move. He needs to learn about his male privilege but I'm
actually talking about real hippos here.

This is the most miserable of all the animal prisons because it's the
largest. The barometer of the modern zoo is based on the spike in penguin
mass suicides, but these places suck anyway so fuck it.

My father, who left me w/ my mother's collections. This exacerbates into
a goat barnyard in the petting area of the park. Both of them are experts at
mannerisms that prevent disclosure.

She has about 30 cookie jars now, ranging from chicken little to baseball
tart. Someday I will have to sort them. I will do something strange to pay
homage to what we couldn't bridge, I will bring the pieces of

ceramic cows and giraffes and rearrange them into a pentagram on the
sidewalk. As a teenager I refused to come home one night and got drunk,
had sex, and passed out. The next day I was sentenced to 2 days

in the county mental health facility. When you picked me up, you didn't
say a word. So the first shard, a piece of a bear nose, goes here

Taupe House

The ugliest cars and the pissiest tree lines. The roundest 24-7 christmas retail shacks. The prissiest teenagers with the most horrible parents with their home drug test kits. They don't stand a chance.

The flimsiest mayoral emergency bunker. The most popular projected war crimes. The sweetest olfactory organs of students as the key to the densest mass uprisings, with or without an ingrown lure.

The most toxic of beta blockers in a 401K run. The smelliest hagiography of her Sunday school sentence, Sister Magdalena is an anxious symptom and streaks only at night across the Burger King parking lot.

The glitziest putz for an ironic banker's wedding. The homeliest Jimmy Choo's worn by jerseys of the world. The latest beat down by rival women outside of the paunchiest boutique motel in Miami, Florida.

The edgiest inaugural rally & the hoodiest American flag cut-offs. The flyest French fry sweaters as an alternative for vegetarians to rock their favorite fast food. The tamest geometrica of skater haircuttins.

The ghostest of the mostest in the MTV graveyard. He slams back his wife's chardonnay as soon as the kids are gone. The securest prepatory school in the eastern seaboard. Now he trains drug sniffing shepherd dogs & doodles bass guitar in a No Wave garage band back in the ladies of his mind.

Navy Blue House

"We are holding your family in prayer," they said, all ironed out in prim dementia lines. The distance of the earn so we read an ode to an urn because a man once said this is required reading. It's a busy day, in the waiting rooms of the world, where talk shows reveal the latest vogue on who to blame if your teenagers are doing drugs. Mexican drug cartels are trending so hard this year.

"From all walks of life, from the inner city to suburbia," says expert. Followed by dandy pits on how to keep your kids locked from the parental unit RX drug cache, that flag must be lighted at all times. The antiphonal babel of blue for boys, and pink for girls. Rainbows signifying they must be snorting mollies off the donkey slide, after eating lunch in the Nutrition Center.

"Any gasoline or backpain?" he's asking for teleconference donations. The prayer request movement is thick: 2 things we feel are inevitable and the latter a planeload of adult eyewitnesses. If someone says they are sending love I don't believe them. That's different from the heart symbol at the end of a letter, you are telling me you are feeling, which is yours.

Lilac House

It's a cashmere easter shrug in the rain. Church is over. Gutter pills
on grandad's side. The rabbit cage named Orville, moaning under a
blush. Pretty.

So she renames him Flaccid. New blood in here, my girl-hammer plebis.
Gnats are snacking on it. Around the turnip of the century, a torro
rave salute.

Ox-blood leather gets better w/ age. In order to fluff her circle skirt.
Beats off w/ boot brush, clawfoot lunch pub on mackerel. It's an old
Gawain gambling,

going to prom so we can sell weed. Two priests performing the beachiest
exorcisms on each other. To add your name, there's a hoop dress store on
third that specializes in tiki cradle cap

Mustard Yellow House

If I said I came here without parents, I'd be lying, if I said I have never entered a room without pictures of you I would be lying, too. I'm afraid to be here because I'm afraid of more family but family is what I need & I suspect we're not the only ones considering what a wooden giftbox means to an American.

The woods need filling. A severing relationship between mother and daughter, son and father. The trees that are cut, the asthmatic cig cold motoring by the eye sockets of a hired hitman tuned logger, out of an unwrapped place where he doesn't have to log until morning, alone. I forgot his name, but

whenever I eat something out of your fridge the taste is stained with old milk & the smell of old milk looks like a winter soldier, where everybody is voting for bookstores that only sell Danielle Steele.

Pine Green House

The dishes suck. The woods do not suck but the dishes do. Doing dishes in the woods sucks. Lights are on in the house. The dishes are done. The dishes still suck. The woods do not suck, ever.

The TV is on. The TV is on because the dishes suck. Do the dishes while the TV is on. The dishes still suck but not as much. The laugh track is fun. No one on TV ever does the dishes. They know the dishes suck.

But there is no TV in the woods. So the dishes suck as much. The firelight is on at camp. The dishes suck in the dark. The woods are dark and do not suck, but the dishes really suck in the dark.

Who does the dishes. The dishes suck. I do the dishes. The dishes that suck when the light is on in the house. The woods do not suck because the woods have no dishes. During firelight or dark,

We avoid the dishes. The kids are gone. We make the dishes. We watch the dishes because the dishes suck. There is a room with TV where there are no dishes. We leave the light off but the dishes still suck

But the woods, as always, do not suck. We buy dishes so doing dishes in the woods will not suck. But you know what? The dishes we bought really suck. They are made of woods so we will do the dishes

Fandango House

Welcome to subverbia. She is wearing a rhinestone cake dress. They usually do. Under the dress is a pair of laurel cowboy boots, hot from line dancing from the rehearsal dinner at a downtown LA hotel.

He, of course, is trident-wielding. They will file the grand kiss and he will imagine diddling the photographer. A wine white wig for the carriage press. The red woods smile down in glee tuileries. People will "like" Halloween candy as a reason to get up in the morning.

Someone is directing the interstitial traffic toward the big game while the press is braying on the diet scale of conviction. They believe in the economy. The bridesmaids are allowed to wear yoga pants only if their thighs don't touch.

Seafoam House

The cat pissed in the toolbox. The cat pissed on the waterbed. The cat pissed on the shovel. barbie dolls, bike seat, teddy ruxpin & silk flowers

The cat pissed on the uniform. The cat pissed on the hot curlers. The cat pissed on the curtains. wallet chain, baseball card, eyeglass case & amber

The cat pissed on the lamp. The cat pissed on the answering machine. The cat pissed on the mop. jade bolero, secret porn, bible study & pogs

The cat pissed on the pager. The cat pissed on the maillot. The cat pissed in the sandbox. light brite, beachball, pool cue & fake nose ring

The cat pissed on the tree skirt. The cat pissed on the flypaper. The cat pissed in the wheelbarrow. flannel pajamas, word search, easter candy & donkey clock

The cat pissed on the lifejacket. The cat pissed on the rug. The cat pissed on the balcony. shamrock beads, trivial pursuit, aqua socks & pickle

The cat pissed on the modem. The cat pissed on the locker. The cat pissed in the carwash. rope licorice, autographed baseball, string cheese & mascara

The cat pissed on the trough. The cat pissed on the roundabout. The cat pissed on you. graham cracker, rhododendron, police hat & lettuce

Bole House

There are reddening sumac leaves in the apex of the ends. So I built my first fire where the heads on the wall are stuffed w/ glass eyes of the folks who stuffed them.

I brought in logs for the fire. They did not fit so I made them fit. I felt arrogant. I am learning the secrets of the glass eye & once a deer stood where I am satisfied. There were no walls & there was no stuffing.

When I was done feeling satisfied I thought about the horse who was fitted but not stuffed, who was standing by the road inside a fence. We were looking at the earth turning & I looked at fires where

our dreams still burned, but it's dark now. I wonder if they keep us in a room w/ the bodiless where nightmares begin when the moon waxes violent. Where dreams take aim from greasy birdhouses.

So I went outside. There were crickets hollering across the night to the horses & the woods being cut for fires so the heads went to sleep, keeping one glass eye open, to learn about the secrets of fitted endings.

Puce House

His body rejected the new lung like my body rejected your dick, but here it is anyway, a fresh new track in the mud, filling with rain, & the children of frogs who have nothing to do with you.

A family of young shelleys in A-line dresses & puce beehives in a forest fire burnt to death. They are holding hands, their heights tiered to indicate who is the cosmetically ordered Oscars mother.

A doctor is in the woods. I'm helping him give my cat a hysterectomy but we close her up when we realize she's already pregnant with little fallout cats blooming up for a prop-job airplane.

Since this is a room I'm not familiar with, I am confronted with the curtain of trust: Love, a stranger that plans your future. It's the conversation that continues after you excuse yourself to go to the bathroom at a dinner party.

Linen White House

The mean girls who become liberals and work at non-profits. What do you mean the world keeps rolling, she says. I have absolutely no desire to become the first woman president.

In every small town in America I become an alcoholic. This means your eyes, your clothes, your gym bag, your poverty. Hot poverty for the good news project of Systemic Theology, Inc.

and my name iss floorplans. A tiny tiny alcoholic wasted in the Kitchen Sink where I am small enough to talk to starlings living in the day old bread of ye old sandwich shop. They want in & I want out,

The hope of school, of strangers with strange pieces of paper owned by shareholders. Feel that ssstillness of ending the war with yourself when the war of symbols begins. I guess it's considered

a privilege to be suspicious of education, but you're assuming the poor have no right to criticize with a heightened sense of smell, that your tongue is the only thing that matters, trespassing the skin of knees

Turquoise House

I reached for the turquoise first for my bath. Smoky quartz, the
proliferation of ponds in unexpected places. Behind Wal-Mart underneath
a shelled eye. Raccoons are certainly justified in any sized city, despite an
OCD human with a scotopic broom.

The beyond plop of bats at dusk, an intersection of an apologizing hill.
Calciferous pots of trilling turquenite, howling in cut-off overhauls. I
heard the ping of a new baby artifice, since sounds not pottying in your
poetic monarchy school are poems about the uprising.

The chicory roots hooting at our useless filibuster. The bill, they say, is
going through the house. I have lived here for nine years, privacy, as a
grateful smoke. No cones, no rods, something to measure with. The safe
whistle-poem bludgeoning, I guess

eventually we'll have to get real. I am suggesting ride share programs
for women across state/country lines with a pleasant venom. We match
mothers with their estranged children, we match the ones who don't
want children, everything free of rape, no border patrol, no ultra
sound theocracy,

you get me, lovelies? We're starting to look like a people who are only
used by the past. I look like a woman that has a future & I'm finally
becoming relieved by that

Smoke House

Being vegan is never enough. I don't hate to break it to you.

There's a poster of a young girl. She's wearing an American flag leotard &
smoke is touring out of our mouths. It's supposed to be cigarette smoke

but I like the possibilities of dry ice, like smoking it might have the ability
to remove malignancy in our communities so people could

gambol better, love better, a magma of super piqued boheme antidotes we
could pass along in a game of adult spin the bottle,

& obviously I'm feeling desperate today to imagine these things, since
smoke usually causes lung disease, locks up screaming, is the bedrock
of furs

for a mechanical eagle prance while visiting their local imperiums. But I
wonder about the uses of smoke. To help hide people who are actively &
collectively being hunted,

people that have to pause to go to the bathroom when they forget who they
are & want to make sure they are here, still alive by the kindness of a mile-
marking mirror,

but most of the smoke I see is usually the wrong kind that hides one group
from another group. I have shared many filtered & unfiltered cigarettes
with people,

having or not having the words & veinlets missing to articulate it. Many conversations end the way they begin, windmilling to "I Only Have Eyes for You" in an empty room,

coming back later to write poems on all the balloons. i don't know how it's supposed to collide but I want to dance with somebody & I want to ask you to dance w/ me

& then I want to turn the record over to learn the coda of the B-side & leave the room again.

Being vegan is never enough. I don't hate to break it to you.

Marigold House

I am typing another disembodied voice. I am looking for clothes with flowers on them. I found a nightgown spotted with marigolds, half-off at value village.

I am planting marigolds by the street. Squirrels & rabbits will tolerate them .Maybe if I smile the barrel will be pointed at someone else. It's a hand-watered striptease.

I am a limb of firecracker kids are lighting off. I used to love sparklers. I used to live for a lot of simple things. I used to believe I could call you when I needed you. The porch ferns are wilting.

I am participating. I am listening to a woman talking to herself. She points to margins that academics support their careers on for the other side of town. My new dress is comfortable on a hot day.

I am a nuisance because we have bills to pay. I am a warning signal if I brush my teeth the wrong way. The first time I went to the dentist I was 15 years old because of a drunken accident.

I am not interested in planting my own dinner. They spent a week tabling against the evils of electricity. I wonder if they enjoy sex. I have problems enjoying sex unless I am pintailed on something.

I am reading an essay by an educated woman on poetry. I crawl into my bed at 4 in the afternoon to watch a drama about affluent lawyers. I switch it off when their world becomes smaller than mine.

I am still thinking about marigolds. They are printed on the dress & they might not be marigolds. I am reading about the topknot. I am reading the responses to the educated woman's essay.

I am not a card player and I don't play chess. They are good at playing chess. Marigolds are edible. I am typing another disembodied voice. I am trying another disembodied voice

I am aiming another disembodied voice. Marigolds, with the petals roped off

Harlequin Green House

Our nuances. A snail-thong. The provoked under-thing. The battle court
pledge molting all over the place.

See if I can provoke the country store without laughing. Let's see if the
courtier snaps his gum when nothing goes with anything. Where do they
hide the rope?

How do they advertise when the executioner retires, or quits by an eclipse
of the frontal lobe. We are old friends, the women & the water bearers,

We sit across from each other on land, the rooms of lonely people that I've
loved. I draw a list of hearts so close together,

that our group picture resembles a rosette of flowering brains, the
violence in the things our grandparents say

frog meshed. Not as good as 3oK each for their student loans but he
showed up yesterday next to the hot tub. He was really Fulbright quiet,

here on shark parkway, where Bill Clinton sells biographical fortunes in
the upside-down flamingo suite. The first plastic egg: "UM"

then a dangled string: " I did not grow prisons in the 90's" Sure you did—&
I'm just a tiny MILF fledgling lost on her way to Trader Joe's

looking for fallen pockets on the big bad husbandry road. When he calls &
asks for the minister of the house the inexhaustible need

to undo myself will answer the lit phone by presenting the opposite
moss tire of a language that's patient. We, as members of the ancestral
revenge class

to flummox an already undignified nation, deserve no less

Bleu de France House

For Seraphine de Senlis

Rain on the shim window of a car I don't know how to drive, my dear. The elephant pleasure of the waterface & it's very un-HUAC of me to love many people at once, the little shits.

Holding camp in the middle of a city owned by hotels, she decided to wear taffeta. Her muses paid the bill to the dressmaker when she knocked on all the village doors, leaving wicks of gas heap clutter.

I do not believe she went willingly. I do not believe her muses were in bed with HUAC sympathizers, even though this happened decades later, I REALIZE this, but the same sentiment was there

that women who listen to the unseen must be hidden in the white breastpockets of the breastless, shamed by a mental health facility nurse with a jesus tattoo on her ankle. Whether it's a cop car

or a wooden wagon led by overworked horses. Whether it's a locked neighborhood in Watts or a detention center for neglected girls. We still paint flowers. We still paint poems.

I do not believe she went willingly. Neighbor, our hearts pumped blood in the same room looking onto lakes that teenagers willingly drown in.

Cerulean Blue House

The laundry also sucks. The laundry sucks but clothes do not. They hide bodies and work hard at receiving and sending identity regalia. So clothes become heavy with things we want and do not want. The laundry sucks because laundry is from a House of

Shaking in the tarot of the sad pitbull. Who wants to remember the night of sad pitbull or the daddy longlegs with no legs. I want to remember but the past is expensive, some never finish watching people wearing memorial dresses, little wires, the laundry clicks with winter pears in our pockets,

The laundry sucks my time from me. But no matter, I am tired of invoking yesterday but I am also lazy. I like people watching, I like watching people play drunk tank. The community washes its clothes because the little person on the tricky bench is happy. I am not happy, I have piles of laundry. Piles at my house,

There's no earth shaking when people are watching me fold clothes. I am seriously putting away what I wear to your house. A dress becomes a test again after being in laundry. Purgatory is being black-out drunk, and the community drinks together on the street. Some people never make it. They itch their

tattoos in the sunlight after the 2 hour rain shower where the people who aren't afraid of water played. I sat this one out. I became heavy with things I want & do not want, I bought my son a pipestone figurine of a coyote to put in his pocket. So far, no bodily abuse. But many people watch us on stilts from tricky laundry habits. Smells are lazy when it comes from a box and it will not keep me from breaking out if I wash my laundry in the wrong coat of a relative. The water in the drunk tank is filling bodies & I hope the new puppy shakes her raincoat off on the crowd playing with their pocketbooks

Cinereous House

Hospitals. Lighted for end times. They run on glossy generators & backup generators, lights of all dreams. If I want to, I can turn the mainland OFF when I want to go to sleep, but the hallways will be a lantern underneath the door so the nurses can find my room during a tornado warning. All I have to do is push a button which has a light next to it & I am able to perceive professionalized help. It's your job to keep me alive in the palace of housing where lights fade into lights, earning their lives from channeled sounds of alert according to a scheduled dose. Time to call for maintenance. I've been meaning to ask if I am foolish to be so grateful. I am after all, fundamentally afraid of people when the majority of them have the potential to hurt me.

Most of us are born here & then placed on silver ashtrays. Floured in a gangled afterbirth ranging of knee-split reds, a purple address bulked across the skull from the cord wrapped around my neck. The primordial first perfumes, born into disinfectant, are housed immediately. Both the moans of new mothering & tingling brown awareness are a force of evidence, searching for a new body through the biohazard wheel. I can relate to the displacement of placentas that have passed through this house. They comfort me. I am fabled in baby blankets when she puts little hats on my head knitted by the widower working in the giftshop.

When people are moved they cry. At least you do when you manage to visit me on Thursdays. But I don't know who's doing the moving. I used to watch the ducks when I started to feel unwell but there is a danger to that because I wasn't sure if they were real or a nervous updraft of self-defense. What do you look like when you allow yourself to be moved. I sat next to the person in the call center with the most sarcastic voice. We are all parrots being paid to speak about histories of past owners. For people we don't see we offer assistance. Professionalized help. I push the light on the screen & someone can read what I am saying.

Candy Apple Red House

Choose a muse. Fall in love with everyone at once. A dog. A cat. A weimaraner. One grey hair when the waiter brings your snotty tapas lunch. My muse & I want to eat a sandwich. Where can we be safe from passive-aggressive politics?

Choose a valuable customer. My muse chooses my doctoring for me. I will finally know how to drive a car so I can pick-up hitchhikers. Burn a house down. I love that you are turned on by a burning house. The alderperson says, "Together we will build a better community".

Choose a witness-relocation program. I'm not a fucking snitch. Pour a glass of water & fall in love with the fish that used to live in it. The muse asks about the co-exist stickers on cars outside the mason-dixon line of the city. "Is this a joke?" She frowns. "If it is, it's in bad taste."

Choose a raccoon. Raccoons are misunderstood. We collect the tails of past deceits & laugh at ourselves. When their hands look so much like ours we feel an irrational competition. I'd like to be in a broken elevator with you so please don't call the animal shelter. She's just sad

Choose an opera glass. Parakeets make the best erasure poems by shitting on the newspaper at the bottom of the birdcage. I'm still strung out on fashion magazines so I want us to be safe

I want us to be safe. Neighborhoods, full rose-reactionary, impotent skylines in the morning. Signs that say "Muses Not Allowed " on lapels, hotel keys, hairbrush handles & jumpsuits

Let's choose again, says my muse. Gently. She's tactful when my neuroses get the better of me but when people believe in dog parks I lose SLEEP I lose sleep I LOSE sleep

It's understandable

Castleton Green House

Think of all the gun suppliers who want to shoot me because time is hideous. They make houses for their guns made out of carpenters. Then they find a reputable glass-man to fit gas over my face.

"We'll take it from here," says the chief of police. They found my body stunning & practical for the town forum. They carry me there so I can co-hair while playing House, show 'em how it's done, Emma's

mom in her lace last silkworms of the world screenprinted across her bag. Anyone can wear a flower crown except for a flower. Hope is soaring today, the different kinds of spears, to undertake manage &

manipulate. "They cut you & send you home," she said. "They insert a piece of cement into one of the vertebrae disks using a small incision."

Aquamarine House

A shiny shiny delicious pistol under the bed in the new new house. Next to
the new new ocean clean of the little shiny t-shirts. Big cholera stampede.
We raise praise a shiny knife. In salut of factory wine

the same time you shoot a little guy of the sea filled with tiny tiny babies,
the bright chlorine sea which is home. The flashy star cameras, top brass,
the t-shirts with shiny knife fights cut into his guts &

the stars come out only as pistols. They are running running a 5K
marathon on the beach splashing on the whalebone ladies posing on the
boardwalk with aquamarine colored drink drinks celebrating

they touch and say goodbye what if the stars don't recognize him the stars
he does not call them, just tiny beings without knives or delicious pistols
or math teachers preparing future future nuclear

animals not trained to do your call of duty dirty work his belly is empty of
sand & now so is the sea, the sea is a marriot courtyard pool with dead little
guys & someone is paid to come out with a net

To net the bleeding gills so not to offend the beachfront property that rises
rises in monetary value next to a clean clean ocean. big star stampede. We
praise raise a shiny knife. In salut of factory pistols

delicious gates to keep out tsunami babies the same time you shoot a little
girl who has never seen the sea which she dreamed could be her home .
They are running running away from the aquamarine

but we stay when we are stars made out of top brass & nuclear marathons
drinking wine on our beachfront property that keeps rising rising rising
next to an ocean of cholera marriotts wearing shiny

shiny little t-shirts posing for the flashy star cameras, the math teacher
preparing us for war pools emptying of little animal babies, their tiny tiny
guts emptied out onto the sandy whalebone floors

Glitter House

Has nothing to do with you. I was going to say. I was going to say social
thing. Social thing like pleather it's a big one, shame. I wish we could go
back & witness our friend's births. What kind of scream or

whimper micromanages you. Traces of languages, a baby with a gourd in
my fist, covered with names. To be shameless with a shovel. Digging up a
stage in a community theatre. If we knew what we were

getting ourselves into. The humanity of a people on the cover of Vogue, a
basketball player next to a supermodel. I feel so good about my progress
that I've fallen in love with life. Like no one else on earth

they say the rich typhoon will be merciful. The shame of an abused people,
the abused people making wars. I may be making you uncomfortable. You
might cough or rattle off laundered seasons of impunity

but I'm way ahead of you. I will open a show called "Angst in Young
Millenials, a Retrospective" sponsored by a hip natural detergent. It will
smell as fresh as an English daisy in a springtime garden

you will walk away with one postcard of the young millennial of your
choice. Feel free to use it as a smart & inexpensive way to dress up your
refrigerator. Everyone deserves to feel inspired, right?

Right. Now If you'll step through the double French doors my team of
international students will be happy to assist you.

Artichoke Green House

The past is the most profitable thing about me. Houses of toys, the samovar is bubbling from the newest river they named after thee. I am no god. I do not wear a confederate shirt to the birthday parties, I am just a kid playing with funny looking reindeer shadows.

You have to make an opportunity pitch. Sidling up to a postcard of women borrowed from time. They sat around and talked. Soon there will be vending machines in the desert and you can access them by a factory-made handicraft, a social capital card that doesn't exist. It's called the future,

it's not really called anything. But then, the standing in for something. I have children that need lunches in the morning so I love them best. I also love lipstick and Europe, and the things that dead men say. We smush the jelly into the summer sausage, it might taste strange at first, but we can make a force

that matters on the online jockeying pad. It runs around the room , everyone who owns a train set. I wash stockings and the elf on the shelf glares at me. He wants me to stop writing as I assign thoughts to someone's caveat, this fantasy four-star review. I'm broke and I'm endearing, I'm lazy and joyfully

dangerous, I am doing exactly what I was shaped to do. The process of weaving objective centerpieces that add a touch of Cape Code reconstruction. Great grandmother Calpurnia secretly wrote a book when the Great Lawyer left for the office. She gave it to me when the elf on the shelf wasn't looking and now the future exists again, only if I cut it up. On his right knee is a long radiowave of a birthmark, that's where it's been determined by DNA evidence that the first human crawled out of the culture club where I've worked as a valet for 35 years. They finally found him plugging quarters into an abandoned village made entirely out of Andy Warhol silkscreens.

Cranberry House

The diversity talking-point chain gang. The delicate warbler, where a
certain carpet will be uncovered before the show tonight, in the newest
crowd-scourge theme of the season: anarchism and artifice.

We'll be adding the local color during the show, rockin ombre hair. Boiled
until the skin falls off. More agreeable as potash bones blinking in the
direction of the ladle. Maybe they won't see us as rookies,

this alembic day for pagination. Not as kings but that's my daddy the
human needling countries that need our help, avenues pleading for
threaded eyebrow lashings. So in my anger (yes I said "anger in a

poem") I go to the 3rd floor without using the escalator (That should make
your health coach happy)a mall which overlooks all the world's gibbeting
with the plush of a hundred stuffed animals. What are

you waiting for? With a mop soaked in red paint I walk past a build a bear
workshop where the dancers are counting off their steps to the tune of the
most popular negation pattern, wearing dresses with

the numbers of the puissant dead. Remember how she would crank your
hospital bed when your back went out and when you told her to stop she
laughed? A must have riposte for the person who owns

the holiday junket kiosks below. But my dear, I am moving quickly, I
needed the release of old cells, old facts. All the blood I am carrying with
me, waterfalling out of the janitor's bucket. I am sick to death of

cleaning up after your mess that isn't supposed to be permanent, the swelling replicas of twisted remakes. Every morning I open those doors but today I am not opening a goddamn thing

Peach House

Peachy as puke. The misery of a public people inside the morning. Scatter, terrier. I need to go to the K-Mart snackbar of my youth. Here is a place where I don't recall buying a R Kelly cassette single, but

I am feeling especially public today in anticipation of my own lunch hour. A lolling hot dog. The sour squelch of Louboutin platforms as they isolate the refrain, pay period switch of a bonemeal basket.

You want me to hide that garbage can for you? When you throw up the pizza you just ate on a hangover & you feel bad about wasting money. This time it stays down. Throw money on you & my body is yours

a nutra bullet of Good Hard Warfare. Cuties & clementines all over the place, the smell of hot meat broth product on an apricot splattered chair. A slow irruption of heel-hoof pimp mansions, the site of

every dream girl's first date. Stopping at the pharmacy first, acne ampules rattling in the rearview mirror from the sub-woofers in your parent's champagne colored Buick. Thank god for concealer

thank god I got a ride to work this morning. Slipping off my old food uniform that smells like stained chicken, you kick me in the grass with my mother watching. I am learning how to be a man.

Sable House

Lumber town. So many lumber houses. That's me, half-caste in the backseat. Mother, let's go for a drive after fishing, to the Upper East Side. The hills that are over there, where architecture is for the golden. I am little & I still believed dreaming about a big house supports a big life,

like the dollhouse kits at Pope's Hobbyland. We could not keep it together, mini chifforobes in my childish mitts cost money & we have no insurance in town where there are also many insurance houses in the stacks. The heart doctor's house is rumored to have its own elevator.

It feels like a landmark siege. The gargoyles skimming from the dentist's piazza to light my mother's cigarettes. We've seen how their owners are winning the discussion in closed conference, but I don't think I've seen anyone open the door at night, heads of fortune space

the negative inglenook of family we are not allowed to muss. But he's allowed to tap my teeth & she's allowed to shock my heart & the neighbor next to him can draw up legal papers in case any teenagers are ambitious for an early emancipation. Surely I cannot afford a lawyer when

he owes us so much money that he's become untouchable. I wonder if their house has an indoor pool. Grandma used to reupholster furniture for the couple that lives there now. Ming things in the foyer that you push boulders in front of before having company, their family

secrets sewn into the livery at the bottom of the hill. That summer a man started cutting up women's faces in the laudromats next to the trainyards

& gravel roads. The man who lives nearby is shabby with downtown financial goals. We named him War Pig since he plans for undesirables,

we latchhook the velvet pillow for their flinty business feet. Years later, I saw one of the women who survived. Sipping coffee where she belonged at Burger King, the one by his office where a man was sitting naked in a booth & refused to leave. The cops left her alone.

Auburn House

He was coiled inside a lake of cerebrospinal mustangs when they dragged him to the surface before his sight was sealed. Afterwards, he could not read at home without a projector.

He wore cowboy boots when he came to visit & the strongest people lifted his chair into the house. The skin of his back surgeons could not dulcify, his disconsolate spine exposed.

Since he was one step above me in the family race saga, he lowered my name to the ground. A bisected baseball park where my mother produced midway babies, so goes the joke even he

was allowed to smirk at. He spoke slowly, separating his words & had a cardboard cut-out of Barbara Mandrell in his Minneapolis apartment. Towards the end of his life he started making

paintings of germinating colors that moved under his breath when he talked into the telephone. He would call my house in the evening, wanting to chat with our grandmother

through the long distance cords. He sent her a painting & for years it hung over the answering machine in the dining room of the apartment she rented. It's in a different place now since

she moved back to the house I grew up in. Next to the painting is your high school senior picture. I look at them when I come for a visit.

Willpower Orange House

Kids from rambrackle houses. An elm street paring knife shared house. Teacher with a loud voice name drops anglo-philosopher gods like lice, strings on the plebs real good.

Hey stuntman in the double barracks. Yeah you. Come down to the center of the jack-in-the-pulpit. This is bad kid school. Draw straws. You live here, my guileless mud dumplings,

donating your body to political science. Afterwards you'll eventually be cremated when we're finished with you, but we don't know when that is, could be a year, 12 years, 25 years,

so there's not really any closure. People who spread their taste for state magic don't write poems about being frightened. I learned at an early age children burn as easily as adults,

the hardest part is practicing how to line up quietly at the door. Hell's bells, here comes a fire officer. He wants to teach which drugs will incinerate our insides & how he will arrest us

if we get caught. How cute is that? Children in jail. What could've been an anti-city of strobelights where kids ruled themselves if you didn't have yr tasers and rot guns. So I'm sure making us watch live video

coverage of the ATF seizing your house was perfect for the pro-war curriculum. Clinton was president. It's still being disputed who started the fire where 17 children died.

Cadet Blue House

Such a helpful bones-errific I've become. Ding ding ding! Satellite windchains. Compare me to bell hooks one more time. Can I borrow your teakwood limousine to take to school?

All night my dreams were political thrillers about marplotting poets. There are elegant men wearing collared shirts. * They're vague about what they want with their violence so I shot

them. Dear premieres of doctoral love, maybe you & I can work on making that plane sound when they carry new politicians to the spank-nag mess hall. I can't imagine a better

javelin gesture than a clock with names on it that swear in Marxism from the highest, wooliest mead-pour. It's like having your own pilot show, eh? A prim-proper glass of cat cribbage.

I really really admire you. A true story of a fierce mother, summer cowcatcher, oh! Look up. Computer running in the room. There is multi-media knowledge being imparted to students

---

* let's keep going with this one: on the stageporch the night Obama was elected, there was over a million pictures posted on Instagram that featured groups of affluent kids throwing up gang signs at George Washington University. You speak slowly to me, you're convinced I can understand obscure references in German. A rose wrapped around a rose bottle filled with Hamm's. I'm as gentle as they come, if I'm not wearing a caftan. The next time I am wearing a poodle skirt with a Gettysburg collar to make you feel comfortable in our gazebo. You had such pretty, copacetic pupils

waking up from sleeping in the same dream. Two poets are trying to cook a whole chicken on the stove. Why don't they cut up the chicken first? Maybe that's supposed to be my job &

they're afraid they might be racist if they ask me. I believe you're supposed to hit your pride before you pass it. There's just one catch: if I help you, I don't want to see any Frank Ocean

or Drake postings as proof that you've passed into the other language. We know you haven't. Set the oven for 350 degrees to bake for the brownest, crispiest skin.

Beau Blue House

Well I declare. Rebranded coliseums, Mazdas for the Romans. I smell gas on your breath. It's never too early for colanders of hairshirt powder.

I smell very strong in the afternoon, on my showering fast. Without it, I'd be an indifferent passerby wearing Laura Ashley organdie,

for my folks at the Dixie-Doxie club. A short traipse to volley in the open air. Guilt as fine as ever, minnows in hot silted water. They are praying for me. I'm a regular,

I live in a shotgun house behind people who say I should perform abortions, if I was so inclined about the welfare of women

but here is a bucket loaded with bait. Coming forth to tip you over. Coming here to save you from eating yourself, they say, out of love.

Russet House

Whenever I smell Jovan musk I think of my great aunt, standing in front of the big picture window. She's expecting company. It's us, we have pulled into the driveway,

Eventually somebody plays a piccolo to invoke robust feelings about an adventurous past. When mom hears a plane overhead she gets goosebumps. "Flying must be in my blood."

My left thumb trembles. Either my will is growing or shirking under the cushions. Holding your thumb habitually under your index finger means your will is broken, says a young witch.

We are next to a recreational airport. The well-off play happily today, weather cooperating on their day off from office. I can hear them spangling their engines underneath the carpet noise

we are making here, of guessing when to compliment & segue into conversations without being direct. By beautiful I mean the exercises we use to disguise it, the merry sailor-suited

clay bear of our efforts. We have diet sodas for the next sublimation, a wistful man sitting in a reproduction Viking ship somewhere in the united states. "I must've been a Viking in a past

life," he says, "because I have a bottomless love for travel." Guarding a demure puppy clucking, we all agree it's high time for the next door neighbor to prune those yellow rosebushes

My House

Holding hands, holding bees. Holding grog for the monkscloth, holding cameras fact-checked in monkscloth. Holding friendships that get you killed. Holding babies.

Holding ferrets at the entrance. Holding passels of fugue. Holding old tortures, holding new ones. Holding people you've never seen in your mind.

Holding Mammy's red petticoat. Holding the whips to my funeral buggy. Holding Biggie. Holding noodle water. Holding a reel of smuggled total control.

Holding the twin bets. Holding how she rocked me. Holding counsel propped with steak dinkus. Holding a butterfly cadaver. Holding nosegays.

Holding a stinkflower. Holding 2 years of paternal contact. Holding the best stories about eating. Holding her electrocuted feet.

Holding what my friend said. Holding what the warden said. Holding what the lecturer said. Holding what the rape maneuver said.

Holding jaws upon jaws, gills upon gills. Holding steel guitars under eurocentric strobe mites. Holding the cow at the killing floor.

Holding the heebee jeebees. Holding ballpark figurines of the dead. Holding perishables. Holding the need. Holding hostis.

Holding a moldy hallelujah . Holding the prolonged successors. Holding a girdle slingshot. Holding your dealings, holding your mood rings.

Holding enemies down by the water. Holding the cloying boys that won't think. Holding the mater dolorosa who slapped the shit out of him.

Holding you in the garage, holding you in the woods. Holding you on the couch. Holding you in the air. Holding you with my best persona non-grata,

Holding you when I feel good enough to get dressed. Holding the dress I took off in the field. Holding you as the professional rollerskater,

Holding you when I'm not capable. Holding all the social cues I've missed. Holding your simulacrums, the conversations that get me going.

Holding the coma belt over old boyfriend territory. Holding a night dream I will never tell you about. Holding all the people that are in this poem,

Holding all the sitcoms I watch on my days off. Holding a folder of fodder factories. Holding tequila shooters. Holding the morning nuptial express,

Holding another day, tomorrow, the next day, your days, the calendar home show. Holding all the walls. Holding all the fusty nails I've swallowed,

Holding my hands across my chest while sleeping. Holding my hands. Holding popular kulture. Holding the last cop in the world. Holding something I'd actually do,

Holding your passive aggressive double joints. Holding their chapters of polite jalopy society. Holding your neo-colonial poetry. Holding your side career of quality control.

Holding my head into a wretched antibiotic. Holding what will kill, exclude, starve, lie, imprison, ignore, deny. Holding the teleprompt applause.

Holding Rejection City, population: every weird black bird. Holding a
party with one good eye. Holding your Brooks Brothers good intentions,

Holding your manhattan pocket square laundered by underpaid
immigrants. Holding the girls in that Robert Palmer video. Holding how
we're all supposed to look like that,

Holding a big fucking saxophone on the subway. Holding decades-
old splinters. Holding friends that want me to stay alive. Holding my
increasing sensitivity about my age,

Holding hot stoves, holding cookstoves, holding cold stoves. Holding
something that is gestural, a sneeze guard mapped around my waste.
Holding jack flaps,

Holding the schoolbuses knitted into your vest. Holding the wood panels
of every memory I have, winking with terrible wuv. Holding your power
snood,

Holding what I'm really saying. Holding how I cuddle my cat. Holding
how I hold it together. Holding another paycheck, a ghost homespun from
spools of watery veal,

Holding all the residual toeholds that are telling me to do this

Acknowledgments

I want to thank the editors of the following publications for giving my poems a home, before they moved to the neighborhood of this book, either in the same versions here or slightly different in both print & audio formats: *Horseless Review, Coconut, Storyscape Journal, Verse Wisconsin, Likewise Folio, Deluge,* Susan Firer at *Shepherd Express, Burdock, Finery, Voicemail Poems,* USA, *Electric Gurlesque Anthology,* & *What's New in Poetry* at *Real Pants.*

I also want to thank the following magical creatures who have been supportive of this book as friends, family, curators, reviewers, & confidants: Laura Goldstein, Jen Tynes, Michael Sikkema, Ching-In Chen, Mike Hauser, Lucas de Lima, Joyelle McSweeney, Sade Murphy, Paul Cunningham, Cynthia Spencer, Andrew Boston, Cassidy Reynolds, Shanna Compton & the Bloof crew, Bruce Covey & the Coconut team, Laura Stokes, Tim Earley, & the poetry community at Woodland Pattern Book Center.

Last but certainly not least, I want to thank my partner Brian Wallschlaeger and our sons, Miles Wallschlaeger & our new little one, Sage Jackson Wallschlaeger. I couldn't have done this without you. Y'all are the best family a girl could ask for. I am grateful.

Nikki Wallschlaeger

is the author of two chapbooks, *Head Theatre* (2007) which etched itself out of her palms unexpectedly & *I Would Be The Happiest Bird* (2014). Her hands continue to talk, which is why she writes. Publications include *Esque, Nervehouse, Coconut Poetry, Word Riot, Pirene's Fountain, Burdock, Spork, DecomP, Shirt Pocket Press, Horse Less Press* and others. She is currently working on a manuscript of poems called *Crawlspace*. She is also the Assistant Poetry Editor at *Coconut*. She lives in Milwaukee with her spouse and son.